Jess Co__

BRATZ™

First published by Parragon in 2007
Parragon
Queen Street House
4 Queen Street
Bath BA1 1HE, UK

ISBN 978-1-4054-8731-3

Printed in China

NEW KID IN TOWN

The Bratz are hanging out in the studio coming up with ideas for the next issue of *Bratz* magazine.

Some solutions aren't that easy. Like this one:

"Dear Cloe, my BFFs and I are crushin' on the same hottie. Help! Signed, Desperate."

In this case I can draw on my own experience. Dear Desperate...

Cloe remembers a situation when a similar thing happened to the Bratz...

Jade loses it.

She falls head-first into a bin and ends up wearing it – a totally wrong fashion accessory!

Quickly forgetting about her tangle with the bin, Jade excitedly tells the others...

But Cloe and Yasmin aren't listening.

They've already spotted the major hottie and are caught in his spell...

... a spell Jade means to break!

Sasha's attempts to steal Shane are interrupted by his phone.

Sasha has an emergency broadcast to make to the others.

Sasha, you can't tell us who to date!

But Sasha is standing firm on this hottie.

I can in this case!

The Tweevils can't believe Burdine is in two places at once. Then they hear something in the toilet.

It's Burdine! But how can it be?

What is it, you annoying minions?

Burdine grabs her shoe to throw at the Tweevils. They get out of there – fast!

Meanwhile, back at the mall...

Back at Burdine's office, Burdine is busy going through her desk.

Suddenly she hears someone enter...

Burdine!

Huh? This isn't Burdine?

Bernice!
What a...
surprise.

The woman behind the desk is Burdine's highly competitive twin sister, Bernice. Burdine is NOT happy to see her.

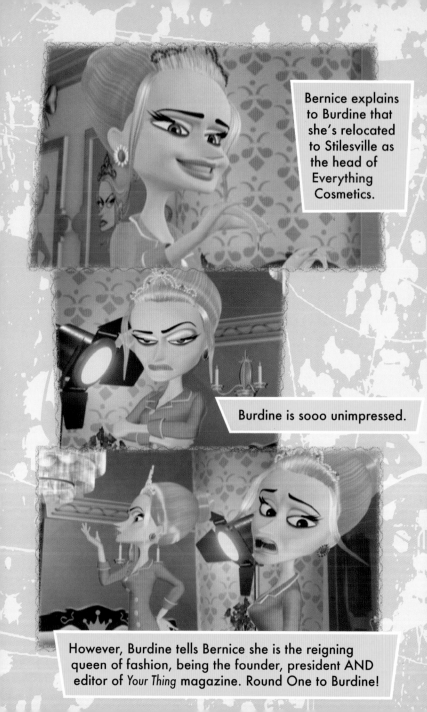

Bernice explains to Burdine that she's relocated to Stilesville as the head of Everything Cosmetics.

Burdine is sooo unimpressed.

However, Burdine tells Bernice she is the reigning queen of fashion, being the founder, president AND editor of *Your Thing* magazine. Round One to Burdine!

ROUND
2

Burdine and Bernice are still at it.
I have two assistants!

Well, I have two interns!

Testing their theory that aliens act weird around appliances, the Tweevils set up a heap of appliances in Burdine's office.

Giggling with excitement, they hurry off to the closet to hide and wait.

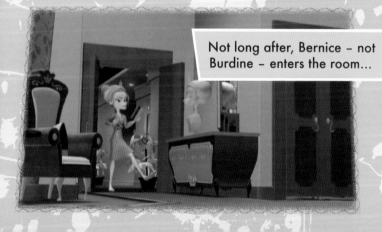

Not long after, Bernice – not Burdine – enters the room...

An automatic vacuum cleaner starts up and moves towards Bernice.

She rides it like a pro until...

Aaaagh!

... the vacuum slams into the walking machine.

And she's off again.

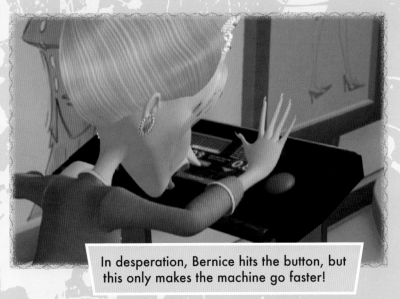

In desperation, Bernice hits the button, but this only makes the machine go faster!

Woa-waaagh!

Bernice is thrown from the walker and lands in a vibrating chair – which vibrates her out of the room!

The Tweevils pop their heads out of the closet.

Burdine really is a total martian!

Wow! Did you like, see that?

The Tweevils freak and run screaming from the office, right over the top of Bernice!

Exhausted from her encounter with the electrical appliances, Bernice flops into the nearest chair.

Aaagh!

But she is soon on her feet again – the Tweevils set her another trap.

Those foolish interns of Burdine's!

Bernice picks up the hot clothes iron left on the chair.

The Tweevils analyze the vibrating chair for traces of alien blood.

Maybe her blood is invisible!

Bernice appears behind the Tweevils, scaring what little sense they have out of them.

Please, don't vaporize us!

... and run straight into - Burdine???

Aaaaaagh!

Where have you two worthless weasels been?! You have a ton of work!

Shane has taken Jade to Pin's nightclub.

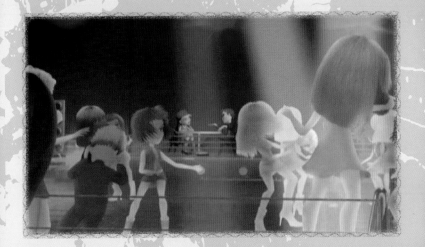

I've never been big on shampoos with built-in conditioners.

Jade listens patiently as Shane discusses his hair.

Needing a little 'retail therapy' Jade heads to the mall with Cloe.

But something catches Jade's eye – something shocking.

I don't believe it!

It's Sasha. And she's out with Shane!

Jade and Cloe CANNOT believe it!

Shane makes his move.

So, tomorrow afternoon?

Guess who's finally up to bat!

Cloe hits a homer!

The Bratz do a little exercise to clear their heads.

A worried Cloe runs in to speak with Sasha.

Sasha finishes her phone call all fired up. She's just been speaking to Dylan. Shane is dating every girl in the school!

He rates them on a scoreboard he keeps in the boy's locker room.

Yeah!

Cameron and Dylan approve.

Apparently Jade and I got 5 stars.

Sasha rallies the troops.

Someone's gotta teach that BOY a lesson!

The Bratz go to work...

Burdine gets ready for the *Entertainment Stilesville* photo shoot.

The REAL star of the family!

The Tweevils arrive to help Burdine prepare.

Cloe and Shane are finally on their date.

Shane is in full game mode, but he doesn't realize he's waaayyy out of his league.

No way, babe! It's you and only you!

Cloe seems to really like Shane, but...

Sorry, gotta take this.

Rrrring!

Shane tries to run from this bad scene but runs into Sasha...

...and then Jade.

Of course it's Burdine – and she gives the Tweevils a blasting to prove it.

Get me and my sister our lunch!

The camera crew arrives just as Kirstee and Kaycee get it...

Sister?!

...but they get it too late to stop their plans from taking effect. Burdine can't stop scratching!

Trying to stop scratching, Burdine pulls Bernice off the desk.

Bernice tries to get away.

Get off me, you impertinent klutz!

The sisters duke it out for the camera. The producer can't believe his luck. This is juicy footage!

Cut!

BRATZ™

YASMIN™

Sometimes Yasmin can be a little quiet, but even without her saying a word, you can sense this girl's special. There's just something about her that seems almost regal. But Yasmin's not pretentious! She's really open-minded – she's always up on alternative trends in fashion, fitness and beauty!
Nickname: Pretty Princess

SASHA™

Sasha's not afraid of confrontation – she knows who she is, what she wants and how to get it! Fashion's a huge part of her life, but music is even more important to 'Bunny Boo!' Someday you can be sure she'll be a record producer... with her own fashion line!
Nickname: Bunny Boo

JADE™

Always on the cutting edge of cool, Jade's the ultimate fashionista! After checking out the latest fashion mags, the trendiest boutiques and all the thrift stores, she always manages to put together looks that are completely unique and just scream 'Kool Kat!'
Nickname: Kool Kat

CLOE™

Cloe's so creative that her whole life has become a work of art, from designing fantastic fashions to creating cool new cosmetic looks to her tendency to be dramatic! Sometimes her imagination runs away with her, but her friends help this 'Angel' stay grounded!
Nickname: Angel